To

Donna

From

Jayne

Date

May 2012

RANDY ALCORN

PHOTOGRAPHY BY JOHN MacMURRAY

~

The PROMISE of HEAVEN

Reflections on Our Eternal Home

HARVEST HOUSE PUBLISHERS

EUGENE, OREGON

To Kathy Norquist, Linda Jeffries, Bonnie Hiestand, Janet Albers, Sharon Misenhimer, Catherine Simons, Stephanie Anderson, Doreen Button, Dwight Myers, Wendy Jeffries, Rebecca Ekstrom, Judy Gettmann, Sandi Swanson, and Sherie Way—the wonderful staff and volunteers of Eternal Perspective Ministries who honor the Lord and are an incredible help to Nanci and me—we are deeply grateful to God for you.

RANDY ALCORN

To all my fellow sojourners, may you catch a glimpse of glory through the beauty of our Father's creation.

JOHN MACMURRAY

CONTENTS

Why Should We Look Forward to Heaven?   7

What Can We Know About Heaven?   11

What Is the New Earth? What Will It Be Like?   21

What Will Our Lives in Heaven Be Like?   31

What Will We Do in Heaven?   47

How Can We Know We're Going to Heaven?   59

Notes   65

INTRODUCTION

How many times have you thought about Heaven in the last week? Unless a person close to you has died, Heaven may not have crossed your mind. But since you have this book in your hand, I assume you want to know more about Heaven.

Everyone has questions about life after death. I've tried to base my answers on what God tells us about Heaven in the Bible.

Heaven is a place where you can live forever someday—a place without fear, anger, sadness, or sickness. It's also a place full of beauty, joy, activity, and rest when you need it. It's a place where you can live with the wonderful and fascinating God who created you. And it's a place where you can meet all sorts of interesting people who will be your friends forever.

I hope you enjoy exploring Heaven in this book.

RANDY ALCORN

WHY SHOULD WE LOOK FORWARD TO HEAVEN?

We are citizens of heaven, where the Lord

Jesus Christ lives. And we are eagerly waiting

for him to return as our Savior.

PHILIPPIANS 3:20

Do I really need to think about Heaven?

~

When I travel, I like to know in advance what it will be like at my final destination. It helps me look forward to the time I'll be spending there. Scripture says, "We are looking forward to the new heavens and new earth he has promised, a world filled with God's righteousness."[1] But we won't really look forward to that place unless we know something about its attractions.

So if Heaven—"the new heavens and new earth"—will be your home someday, wouldn't you like to discover all you can about it now?

Some people have the idea that in Heaven they'll be sitting around on clouds wearing funny clothes, and strumming a harp. They don't look forward to going there because they fear that Heaven will be...well, boring.

It's not. Heaven is a place worth thinking and talking and dreaming about. Once you understand what the Bible says about Heaven, you'll look forward to living there.

WHAT CAN WE KNOW ABOUT HEAVEN?

He showed me the holy city, Jerusalem, descending out

of heaven from God. It shone with the glory of God and

sparkled like a precious stone... The glory of God

illuminates the city, and the Lamb is its light.

REVELATION 21:10-11,23

Is Heaven a real place?

D o you wonder how we can know anything about Heaven—a place we can't see? Well, God has revealed unseen things to us in his Word, including things about Heaven.

Many people doubt that Heaven is a real place. They believe people in Heaven float around like ghosts. But the Bible tells us that Heaven is just as real as planet Earth. In fact, God calls the Heaven we'll live on forever the "New Earth."

We're human beings. We're not made to live as ghosts in a ghostly place, we're made to live on Earth.

If we know Jesus, we will enter Heaven when we die. And some time after Jesus comes back to Earth, God promises he will bring us to live on the New Earth—a world with land, trees, and water: "Look. I am creating new heavens and a new earth, and no one will even think about the old ones anymore."[2]

This place will be beautiful beyond our wildest imagination. That's why this book is full of *earthly* pictures, not what we usually think of as "heavenly" ones. Understanding the New Earth is simple because it will be like the earth we're living on now—only better. So as you enjoy these beautiful photographs taken by my friend John MacMurray, think of them as just a sampling of the beauty of God's coming New Earth.

Of course, there are many things about Heaven we won't know until we get there. On Earth there are pleasant surprises and unpleasant surprises, but in Heaven God will give us only pleasant ones. And he has a lot of them prepared specially for us.

If we're good people, does that mean we'll go to Heaven someday?

Many people believe that everyone who's good will automatically go to Heaven. But the Bible says no one can be good enough to get there. We've all sinned, falling short of God's standards. God's holiness requires that sin be punished, and the Bible says "the wages of sin is death."[3]

Every sinner deserves to die, and we are all sinners.

But Jesus Christ went to the cross to die in our place. Then he came back to life in his same body. His resurrection is very important to our Christian faith. And it's the key that unlocks our understanding of Heaven and what it will be like.

So no one goes to Heaven based on good deeds. We get there only as a gift from Jesus.

God allows us to choose whether or not to trust Jesus. Turning away from our sin and believing in Jesus' death and resurrection is the only way to make Heaven our future home. The Bible says:

> We are made right with God by placing our faith in Jesus Christ. And this is true for everyone who believes, no matter who we are. For everyone has sinned; we all fall short of God's glorious standard. Yet God, with undeserved kindness, declares that we are righteous. He did this through Christ Jesus when he freed us from the penalty for our sins. For God presented Jesus as the sacrifice for sin. People are made right with God when they believe that Jesus sacrificed his life, shedding his blood.[4]

But it's not enough to know these facts. We need to be sure we take God up on his offer of forgiveness. We need to accept—with thanks—his free gift of eternal life, so we can live forever with Jesus. Then we can know for sure that when we die, we will go to Heaven.

What does it mean to store up treasures in Heaven?

Jesus said, "Don't store up treasures here on earth…Store your treasures in heaven."[5]

When we die, we won't be able to take anything with us to Heaven. So God wants us to be more interested in the things that will last beyond this life.

What will last for eternity? Our relationship with Jesus and other people who love him. We store up treasures in Heaven when we get involved with God's work on Earth by serving others instead of spending all our time and money on ourselves. We can use our talents to share God's love with others. By giving and doing things for Jesus now, what is truly important will be waiting for us when we get to Heaven. While we don't know exactly what all these treasures will be, we do know that God is the greatest giver in the universe, and whatever he promises to be treasures will surely be magnificent.

The more treasures you have in Heaven, the more you'll look forward to going there.

What happens to us when we die?

D ead people don't come back and talk about life on the other side. But we can know some things based on what Scripture says. We don't just disappear after we die. We live on in another location. Followers of Jesus go to live with him in Heaven. On the cross, Jesus told the thief crucified next to him, "Today you will be with me in paradise."[6]

Most of this book is about the future Heaven, where we will live forever with God and all those who know Him. That's the place where we'll live after our resurrection and after the end of this present Earth. What do I mean by our resurrection? When Jesus returns to Earth—and he promises he will someday—everyone who knows God will be given a new body.

Usually when we refer to Heaven, we're not thinking about the future Heaven; most often we mean the present Heaven, the place where Christians go as soon as they die.

The present Heaven, however, is not our final destination. Though it's a wonderful place, it's not the place we're made for—the place where God promises we can live forever. That future Heaven is called something you might not expect. It's called the New Earth.

What's the difference between the present Heaven and the future Heaven?

The present Heaven is where angels live and where people who love Christ go when they die. The apostle Paul said that to die and be with Christ would be "far better."[7]

The future Heaven will be the home of God's people who now live on Earth and in the present Heaven. And God himself will live with his people there.[8]

Some might think that the New Earth shouldn't be called Heaven. But Heaven is whatever special place God decides to make his home. Since God promises he will make the New Earth his dwelling place, and have his throne there, that means the New Earth will be Heaven.

Because it's a real earth, that New Earth won't seem strange to us. It will be our home. It will be the very best of this Earth and more.

WHAT IS THE NEW EARTH?
WHAT WILL IT BE LIKE?

Then I saw a new heaven and a new earth...

And I heard a loud voice from the throne saying,

"Now the dwelling of God is with men, and he will live

with them. They will be his people, and God himself

will be with them and be their God..." [Jesus]

said, "I am making everything new."

REVELATION 21:1,3,5 NIV

Is God going to destroy the Earth and make a completely different one?

Peter, one of Jesus' twelve apostles, wrote about what will happen someday: "The heavens will pass away with a terrible noise, and the very elements themselves will disappear in fire, and the earth and everything on it will be found to deserve judgment."[9]

Some theologians think the Earth will be completely destroyed and a different Earth will be made from scratch. But the Bible teaches that while the Earth will be destroyed, it will also be restored. God will remake the remains of the old Earth into a much improved New Earth.

It will be the same way with our bodies which now die and decay. God will bring them back to life and better than new.

This Earth is broken because of sin. But Jesus is going to fix it, just as he's going to fix those who love him. We'll be the same people made new, and we'll live on the same Earth made new because God will remodel it and we'll inhabit it with him.

Will the New Earth be like our Earth was in the beginning?

The Garden of Eden was breathtakingly beautiful. The first people God created lived there in the days before pollution, earthquakes, wars, poverty or crime. We can only imagine what it was like.

We should expect this New Earth to be like the Garden of Eden, only better. That's exactly what the Bible promises.[10]

All our lives, even if we don't know it, we've been dreaming of the New Earth. Whenever we see beauty, it reminds us of our eternal home—it's a sample of what's to come, and should make us think about living on the New Earth.

The New Earth will still be Earth just as we, in our new bodies, will still be ourselves. So we can expect New Earth's sky to be blue and its grass green. Lake Michigan will likely become New Lake Michigan, and Niagara Falls the New Niagara Falls. Some of our favorite mountains, meadows, deserts, forests, lakes, waterfalls, and camping spots may be there.

We will see things the way they were meant to be. Everything we love about the old Earth will be ours on the New Earth. Once we understand this, we won't regret leaving all the grand places we've seen or wish we'd seen. We know we'll see many of them on the New Earth—and they'll be better than ever.

24

What will the New Jerusalem be like?

The New Jerusalem will be the New Earth's capital city—the largest city ever. It will be a huge garden city, more beautiful than any other.

John describes the city this way: "The wall was made of jasper, and the city of pure gold, as pure as glass. The foundations of the city walls were decorated with every kind of precious stone."[11] There will be more wealth in this immense city than has been gathered in all human history. Everyone will be free to enjoy it, and no one will ever fight over it or try to keep it from others.

An angel tells John that the New Jerusalem is 1400 miles in length, width, and height.[12] A city this size in the middle of the United States would stretch nearly from Canada to Mexico and from Salt Lake City to Chicago.

It appears there will be many other cities on the New Earth, since Jesus said that in the Kingdom some would rule over five cities and some over ten.[13] But no city will be like this great capital city—and there on Main Street, in the center of the city, will be "the throne of God" and his Son, Jesus, the King of kings.[14]

Who will rule the New Earth?

When God created the world, he decided that humans should rule the Earth: "God blessed them and said, 'Be fruitful and multiply. Fill the earth and govern it. Reign over the fish in the sea, the birds in the sky, and all the animals that scurry along the ground.'"[15]

Human kingdoms will come and go until Jesus sets up a kingdom that forever replaces them. Someday he will be declared the absolute ruler of the universe. He will turn over to his Father the Kingdom he has won,[16] and then God will give people the responsibility to rule the New Earth.[17]

We will lead people like us. And angels too. "Don't you realize that someday we believers will judge [rule over]...angels?"[18] We will also rule animals, just like God told Adam and Eve to do in Genesis 1–2.

And who will lead us? Other people. In any government, people are both over and under other people. On this Earth, we sometimes think serving others is a burden. But on the New Earth, it won't be. There will be no pride, envy, boasting, or other sinful attitudes.

How long will God's kingdom last on the New Earth? God gave the answer to the prophet Daniel: We "will rule forever and ever."[19]

Does God have plans for animals on the New Earth?

The Bible tells us that animals were an important part of God's creation. "God made all sorts of wild animals, livestock, and small animals, each able to produce offspring of the same kind. And God saw that it was good."[20]

Animals weren't created in God's image, and they aren't equal to humans. Still, God created animals and cares about them, which means we should too. Animals were important in Eden, when the Earth was perfect. So they'll probably be important on the New Earth, where everything will once again be perfect.

Will we see our pets again on the New Earth?

God is the giver of all good gifts. So if it would please you to have your pets on the New Earth, that may be a good enough reason for God to make it happen.

It seems reasonable to assume that God could do one of three things on the New Earth: (1) create entirely new animals; (2) bring back to life animals that have suffered in our present world, giving them new bodies that will last forever; (3) create some new animals *and* bring back to life some old ones. God talks about one day rescuing not only people, but the rest of his creation that suffers now. [21] That suggests some animals now living will live again. These could, it seems to me, include our pets. Wouldn't that be great?

I imagine that extinct animals and plants will be brought back to life. By resurrecting his original creation, God could show his complete victory over sin and death. Animals were created for God's glory and to show us what God is like. What could speak more of his awesome power than a tyrannosaur? These animals were part of a world he created and called "very good." So why wouldn't we expect God to include them when he remakes the world?

WHAT WILL OUR LIVES IN HEAVEN BE LIKE?

You will show me the way of life,

granting me the joy of your presence and

the pleasures of living with you forever.

PSALM 16:11

Will we become angels in Heaven?

People and angels are very different. If you live in Heaven, you will still be human. God loves variety, and he doesn't make all intelligent creatures alike.

Angels are beings with their own identities. They have names, like Michael and Gabriel. Under God's direction, they serve us on Earth. The archangel Michael reports directly to God, the other angels serve under Michael. In Heaven, human beings will be in charge of angels.[22]

Will we have feelings and express them?

In the Bible, God is said to love, laugh, take delight, and rejoice, as well as be angry and sad. We know that after Jesus' friend Lazarus died, "Jesus wept."[23] God also tells us that when the disciples tried to send some children away from Jesus, "he was angry with his disciples."[24]

We were made in God's image, so we have feelings and express them just as God does. We should expect to do the same in Heaven.

On Earth we sometimes allow our feelings to lead us into doing wrong. Anger, for example, can prompt us to hurt other people or feel hurt by them. In Heaven we'll all be free to feel deeply and never have to fear that we'll hurt anyone. We'll love each other with pure hearts.

I really look forward to that.

Will we be allowed to have or do what we really want?

We'll have many desires in Heaven, but everything we want will be good. Our desires will please God. He created our desires and all the things we long to have. When we enjoy looking forward to the gifts God has promised us, we're enjoying him.

One of the best things about Heaven is that the sinful desires we had to fight on Earth won't be around anymore. We'll enjoy food without eating too much or too little; we won't do anything to hurt ourselves, and we won't do anything to hurt others.

On the New Earth there will no longer be a difference between what we *ought* to do and what we *want* to do.

34

Will we have the same identities we have now?

You will be you in Heaven, and I will be me.

The risen Christ did not become someone else. When he appeared to his disciples after his resurrection, he told them, "You can see that it's really me."[25] He was the same Jesus he had been before.

Our personalities and histories will continue from the old Earth to the New. So you'll still recognize friends and family and they will recognize you. Best of all, Jesus will know you...and you will know him.

While some people say that in Heaven we will no longer be male or female, the Bible doesn't say that. When people saw Jesus in his resurrection body, they knew he was still a man. Likewise, we will still be the gender we are now.

What will our new bodies be like?

After Jesus comes back to this Earth, we'll have new bodies for the New Earth. And these bodies will be better than anything we can imagine. For one thing, they will be free of the curse that came upon Earth because of the first sin in the Garden of Eden.[26]

The curse removed beauty from God's creation. God promises on the New Earth, "No longer will there be a curse upon anything."[27] So without the curse, everything and everyone God has made will be beautiful. And we'll never fail to see that beauty in them. There will be no diseases, no disabilities, no tragic accidents.

God will decide how our perfect bodies will look, and there's no reason to believe we'll all look alike. Different heights and weights seem as likely as different skin colors. God is the Inventor of variety. We'll be perfectly happy with the way God makes us.

Will we ever be tempted to do something wrong?

Because Adam and Eve—who lived in a perfect place—sinned, many people wonder if we'll sin someday in Heaven. After all, Satan was perfect, then he rebelled against God. And didn't he live in Heaven when he first sinned?

The Bible says that in Heaven "there will be no more death or sorrow or crying or pain. All these things are gone forever."[28] It also says that "the wages of sin is death."[29] Because sin always leads to death and sorrow and pain, the promise that there will be no death or sorrow or pain is also a promise that there will be no sin.

The Bible says that God cannot sin. It would be against his nature. Once we are with him in Heaven, we'll share in God's righteousness, and it will be against our nature too.

Will all people get the same rewards in Heaven?

We usually want to be treated equally (unless everyone else is treated badly). In some ways, every person will be treated the same in Heaven. Jesus told a story about some workers who were hired at the beginning of a day and

some who were hired one hour before quitting time.[30] All of the workers received the same pay. But the workers hired earlier complained that they should get more money because they worked the longest. Jesus said if the one doing the hiring wanted to pay some people more than they deserved, that was up to him. No one else had a right to complain.

This story reminds us that all people who believe in Jesus will go to Heaven. This is true for the person who begins to trust Jesus at the age of seven and the one who doesn't trust Jesus until the age of ninety-two. God will love everyone the same. However, they won't all have the same rewards in Heaven.

Most Christians don't talk about rewards, even though the Bible does. Here are a few of the many important things the Bible says about rewards in Heaven:

- ➤ The Lord will reward each one of us for the good we do.[31]
- ➤ [Jesus said,] "I tell you the truth, anyone who gives you a cup of water in my name because you belong to Christ will certainly not lose his reward."[32]
- ➤ "I am the one who searches out the thoughts and intentions of every person. And I will give to each of you whatever you deserve."[33]

Some Scriptures mention that we'll have different rewards and positions in Heaven, according to the way we serve God now. Those who have served Jesus more faithfully on Earth will receive greater reward and responsibility on the New Earth. But in Heaven, we won't complain, "That's not fair." We'll know that all of God's choices for rewards are right. And we'll never envy others or resent them.

Because we know we can never do anything to earn our way to Heaven, we sometimes discount the idea of doing good works to serve God. But the Bible says that even though we can't earn our way to Heaven by doing good deeds, those who are going to Heaven please God with our good works.[34]

Will we know everything?

Only God knows everything.

When we die and go to live with God, we'll understand things more clearly, and we'll know much more than we do now. [35] But even then we'll never know everything. We're not God.[36]

Even angels don't know everything. Just like us, though, they desire to know more.

There's much to discover in this universe, but here on Earth we have so little time and opportunity to learn all the things we want to learn. We'll have plenty of time in Heaven. Among other things, we'll be able to explore the New Earth and discover amazing things about God's creation, all of which will tell us more about our Creator.

We might not understand some events on this Earth, such as why hurricanes happen or innocent people are killed. Yet Paul wrote that "God causes everything to work together for the good of those who love God and are called according to his purpose for them."[37] How's that possible? Because God knows everything and he's all-powerful. In Heaven we'll understand why certain things happened and how God brought good even out of the painful experiences we've had.

One day we'll see God and truly know him.[38] Then things will make sense. We'll never understand everything, but we'll know and trust the God who does understand everything. So we'll never again have reason to worry. And if we realize that God is good and knows all and can do whatever he wants, we don't have to worry now either.[39]

Will we each have our own place to live?

Jesus said, "In my Father's house are many rooms...I am going there to prepare a place for you."[40] This suggests Jesus has in mind for each of us an individual dwelling that's a small part of a much larger place.

That's Heaven: a place both large and private. Some of us enjoy coziness, being alone in a quiet space. Others enjoy a huge, wide-open space. The New Earth will offer both.

Heaven isn't likely to have houses that are all the same. God loves being creative. He makes things special for each of the children he loves. When we see the particular place he's prepared for us, my place will feel just right for me, and yours will feel just right for you. We'll be comfortable and perfectly happy in the most ideal home we've ever had.

Will we spend time just with Jesus, or will we have other friends too?

The best part of Heaven will be spending time with Jesus. While Jesus was here on Earth, crowds followed him because they loved him and wanted to be near him. But unlike most celebrities, he will never disappoint you. Being near Jesus is what will make Heaven what it is—Heaven.

While Jesus will be our best friend, God the Father will be delighted to see us having other great friendships in Heaven too. God said it's not good for people to be alone.[41] He understands our need for friends and our desire for

those friendships to continue in Heaven. He's the one who made us that way. In Heaven we'll have our old friends who know Jesus and many new friends as well.

Will people be married in heaven?

O n the New Earth we will all be one big family, and marriage won't exist in the same way it does now.[42] But the most important thing about a marriage is the special love and friendship that a husband and wife share with each other. That's a picture of the wonderful love and friendship that Jesus and all those who know him will share in Heaven.

When Paul talks about marriage he calls it "a great mystery...an illustration of the way Christ and the church are one."[43] Jesus has proven forever how much he loves us, more than any husband has ever loved his wife. After all, he chose to die on the cross for us. How could we not return that love?

Although Jesus said people won't be married in Heaven, he never said that married people would stop loving each other. Those who had great times together and faced great difficulties together in this life will naturally have close relationships. Families who love Jesus will be closer than ever in Heaven.

43

**If some people we love aren't in Heaven,
won't we experience sadness?**

Sometimes people ask "If God is good, why do some people go to Hell?" The answer is that we are sinners and God is holy. But people can go to Heaven if they admit their sins and trust Jesus to save them. But when someone rejects Jesus, God's Son, that person also rejects God the Father.[44]

Some people you know may choose not to believe in God or obey his teachings. God doesn't force anyone to follow him. But since Heaven is where God lives, to reject God is to reject Heaven. It is home only to those who *want* to be there with him.

In Heaven we'll have a better understanding of what a fair judge God is. We'll know that everything he does is exactly right. Someday we'll see clearly that God gave everyone a chance to know him.[45] We'll be amazed at how many opportunities he gave people to follow him.

Meanwhile, we should pray that our family members and friends will bow their knees before Jesus, confess their sins, and choose to follow him and accept God's gift of eternal life.

One thing we know for certain—any sorrows we have now will disappear forever on the New Earth. The Bible promises, "He will wipe away every tear from their eyes...neither shall there be mourning nor crying nor pain."[46]

This is God's promise. You can count on it.

WHAT WILL WE DO IN HEAVEN?

Blessed are the dead who die in the Lord from now on...

They will rest from their labor, for their deeds will follow

them...The throne of God and of the Lamb will be

in the city, and his servants will serve him.

REVELATION 14:13; 22:3 NIV

Will Heaven ever be boring?

People sometimes say, "I'd rather have a good time in Hell than be bored in Heaven." But Hell is a place where everyone is lonely and miserable, where friendship and good times don't exist. Hell will be deadly boring. Everything good, enjoyable, fascinating, and exciting comes from God. Without God—and all the good things that come from him—there's nothing interesting to do. King David wrote, "You will show me the way of life, granting me the joy of your presence and the pleasures of living with you forever."[47] There is no joy without God, and in God's presence there's nothing *but* joy.

Since Heaven is God's home, made by him, it will be awesome, exciting, and always fascinating. Heaven is going to be full of great surprises and astonishing new adventures as we learn more about God and enjoy his wonders in a new universe. Once we're in Heaven, we'll wonder why we weren't even more excited about going there.

Will we have to work in Heaven?

Heaven is not a place filled with hammocks—one for each person to lie on and rest, rest, rest. Though we will rest, we're told "his servants will serve him,"[48] which means we'll also work in Heaven.

When Adam and Eve disobeyed God, work became burdensome. God told Adam, "The ground is cursed because of you. All your life you will struggle to scratch a living from it."[49]

On the New Earth we won't *have* to work. We will *want* to work. The work we do will be enjoyable. Likewise, when it's time to rest, we'll want to rest. When it's time to gather and sing praises to our God, we'll want to do that. We'll always get to do what we want to do, and we'll always want to do what it's time to do.

We'll be able to do the work started by Adam and Eve: ruling over the Earth for God's glory. When a person enters Heaven after faithfully serving God, he's told by his Lord, "Well done, my good and faithful servant. You have been faithful in handling this small amount, so now I will give you many more responsibilities. Let's celebrate together."[50]

Think about the kind of work you enjoy. When you're working on a hobby, it doesn't seem like work, does it? We'll be just as excited to do our work in Heaven someday as we are to spend time on our favorite sport or hobby on Earth now.

Will we sing, dance, and make music?

Music is an important part of life—something that many of us would be unhappy about leaving behind. The good news is we won't leave it behind. There will be plenty of great music in Heaven. The apostle John speaks of trumpets and harps in the present Heaven.[51] If there are musical instruments in the present Heaven, we can certainly expect to find them on the New Earth where we'll have resurrection bodies.

The Bible is full of examples of people praising God with singing and musical instruments. In the Temple, people sang and played different instruments. The psalm writer instructed people to praise God with all kinds of instruments: string, woodwind, brass, and percussion. Jesus sang with his disciples, and the apostle Paul instructed Christians to sing to the Lord.[52]

Not only will there be music, there will be dancing. Throughout the ages, people have danced to God's glory on Earth. After the parting of the Red Sea, Miriam and the women of Israel danced and played tambourines, singing praises to God. King David danced as he worshipped the Lord. When the Prodigal Son returned home, the house was filled with music and dancing.[53]

God created us with the ability to dance. Just as we can use our voices and musical instruments as a way to worship God, we can also use dancing to honor him.

Will there be art, entertainment, and sports?

Do you like a good movie or play? Maybe you enjoy painting or drawing. It was God who invented art. He's the greatest Artist ever—he created the universe, trees and flowers and waterfalls, dogs and cats and zebras, and people. Then he wrote, directed, and took the leading role in history's greatest story. (It's the Awe-Inspiring Mind-Blowing Drama of Redemption.) He's the one who gives artists and writers the minds and emotions and physical senses that furnish their ideas.

Will we find ways to use the arts to praise God? Will these arts continue to provide enjoyment and entertainment for people? I believe the answer is yes. Since the New Earth will be greater than our present Earth, then surely the greatest books, dramas, and poems are yet to be written.

And what about sports? Have you ever thought you might enjoy your favorite sport when you live on the New Earth with a perfectly healthy body? I can't find a single good reason to believe sports won't be part of our lives there.

God compares the Christian life to sports competitions.[54] Sports and our enjoyment of them are positive things. If people hadn't become sinners, they would still have invented baseball and soccer and competitive swimming. There would probably be more and even better sports than we have today. I love playing tennis, and I think I'll get to do it in my resurrection body. Think about this—your favorite sport may be one you've never even tried yet, but will discover on the New Earth!

Will we laugh?

God created all good things, including good humor. If God didn't have a sense of humor, we wouldn't either. But it's obvious that he does: Think about aardvarks and baboons and giraffes. Take a good look at your dog catching a Frisbee or your cat chasing a ball or an otter at play. You have to smile, don't you?

In Heaven, I think Jesus will laugh with us, maybe loudest of all. His fun-loving nature will probably be our greatest source of endless laughter.

Am I just guessing about laughter? No. Speaking of Heaven, Jesus said, "God blesses you who weep now, for in due time *you will laugh.*"[55]

As we look forward to the laughter to come, Jesus says we should "leap for joy" now.[56] Can you imagine someone leaping for joy in silence, without laughter? Listen to any group of people who are enjoying some kind of celebration, and what do you hear? Laughter.

When life is difficult, remember what Jesus promised about life in Heaven: "You will laugh." You didn't think it was human beings who invented play and fun and joy, did you?

Will we explore the universe?

God promises to make not only a New Earth but also "new heavens," [57] what we can see and beyond.

As a 12-year-old, I first viewed the great galaxy of Andromeda. It contains a trillion stars, far more than the four billion in our own galaxy. We can only guess how many planets there are, and what they're like. As I looked through that telescope, I was in awe of this galaxy. But I knew nothing about God. I felt small and alone. Years later I became a Christian. I found that gazing through the telescope became an act of worship once I knew the God who made this incredible universe.

Since the Andromeda Galaxy is part of this creation, the Bible's promise of new heavens—the old heavens made new—suggests there will be a New Andromeda Galaxy. From the night I first saw that place, I've wanted to go there. Now I think it's possible that one day I will.

God made billions of galaxies containing countless trillions of stars, planets, and moons. The heavens point to God's glory now, and we know we will be praising God forever. So don't you think exploring the new heavens, and ruling over them, may be part of God's plan for us?

Because God isn't limited by time, he may choose to show us past events as if they were happening right now. Maybe God will let us time travel. God might show us how he helped us and watched over us on this Earth. Maybe we'll see how our small acts of faithfulness and obedience changed the lives of others.

We can be sure of this: Whatever's ahead of us, in the new heavens and on the New Earth, it's far better than we can imagine.

Will we be able to fly and do other amazing things in our new bodies?

When Jesus came back to life, he had a new body with some amazing abilities. He suddenly appeared to his disciples in a locked room. He was able to disappear from the sight of two of his followers as they shared a meal together. When Jesus left the Earth, he wasn't held down by gravity but ascended into Heaven.[58]

It's possible that Jesus, who is both man and God, has certain physical abilities that we won't have. However, the Bible tells us that our new bodies will be like his, so we may be able to move and travel in different ways than we can now. We don't know the amazing plans God has for our bodies. Maybe we'll be able to fly like an eagle or run like a cheetah.

Will we eat and drink in Heaven?

Many people believe that in Heaven there will be no need to eat or drink. But after his resurrection, Jesus asked his disciples for some food and ate a piece of fish in front of them.[59] So resurrected people can and do eat real food. We're told the tree of life will grow in the middle of the New Jerusalem, and it will produce fruit every month. We can only imagine how wonderful Heaven's fruits will taste.[60]

Other Scriptures say we'll enjoy feasts with Jesus in an earthly kingdom.[61] And an angel in Heaven told John, "Blessed are those who are invited to the wedding feast of the Lamb."[62]

What do people do at a feast? Eat and drink, tell stories, celebrate, laugh, and have dessert.

HOW CAN WE KNOW WE'RE GOING TO HEAVEN?

I have written this to you who believe

in the name of the Son of God, so that you

may know you have eternal life.

1 JOHN 5:13

The wedding singer and the book

My friend Ruthanna Metzger sang at the wedding of a wealthy man. The reception that followed was on the top two floors of Seattle's Columbia Tower, the Northwest's tallest skyscraper. At the top of the stairs that led to the reception stood the maitre d' with a book open in front of him. He asked each person about to enter, "May I have your name, please?" He would then check his book to make sure the name was listed before admitting anyone.

When Ruthanna and her husband, Roy, came to the door, she gave the man their names.

He searched through his book and said, "I'm not finding it. Would you spell it, please?"

Ruthanna spelled her name.

"I'm sorry, but your name isn't here."

"There must be some mistake," Ruthanna said. "I'm the singer. I sang for this wedding."

"It doesn't matter who you are or what you did," the man answered. "Without your name in the book, you can't attend the reception." He motioned to a waiter and said, "Show these people to the service elevator, please."

Ruthanna and Roy took the elevator to the parking garage, found their car, and drove away disheartened. After a while Roy asked what had happened.

"When the invitation arrived, I was busy," Ruthanna said. "I never bothered to RSVP. Besides, I was the singer. I thought I didn't have to respond to the invitation."

Some people are too busy to respond to Christ's invitation to his wedding banquet. Many think they will get into Heaven if the good they've done outweighs the bad. But people who don't say yes to Christ's invitation to forgive their sins are people whose names aren't written in the Book of Life.[63] And if you aren't allowed into Heaven's wedding banquet, the only other place to go will be Hell.

There won't be any excuse for saying no to Jesus that will be good enough. If our names aren't written in the book, we'll be turned away.

Have you said yes to Christ's invitation to join him at his wedding feast? Have you asked Jesus to forgive your sins so you can spend eternity with him in his house? If so, you have reason to be happy—Heaven's gates will open wide for you.

You don't have to wonder whether you're going to Heaven: "I have written this to you who believe in the name of the Son of God, so that you may *know* you have eternal life."[64]

Do you know you have eternal life? You can.

Living now with Heaven in mind

My wife, Nanci, and I have spent some wonderful moments with our family and friends. Sometimes it's been so good that we've said, "It just doesn't get any better than this." Have you ever had a great moment when you felt that way?

Well, it *does* get better than this. Because no matter how good the very best moments of this life have been, the most ordinary moment in Heaven will be far better.

Do you really believe you will live forever in a place where Christ is the center of everything and the source of all joy? Do you believe that God is using even the difficult times in your life to prepare you to be one of his rulers on the New Earth? Do you look forward to a New Earth "filled with God's righteousness"?[65]

If you do—and I sure hope so—then you'll want to get a head start on Heaven by living for Jesus right now.

If I don't get to meet you here, I look forward to meeting you there, in that incredible world God is preparing for us—a world where every day will be better than the one before.

NOTES

1. 2 Peter 3:13
2. Isaiah 65:17
3. Romans 6:23
4. Romans 3:21-25
5. Matthew 6:19-20
6. Luke 23:43
7. Revelation 21:1,3
8. Revelation 22:1,3
9. 2 Peter 3:10
10. Revelation 22:1-5
11. Revelation 21:18-19 NIV
12. Revelation 21:15-16
13. Luke 19:17,19
14. Revelation 22:1-2
15. Genesis 1:28; Psalm 8
16. 1 Corinthians 15:28
17. Revelation 22:5
18. 1 Corinthians 6:2-3
19. Daniel 7:18
20. Genesis 1:25
21. Romans 8:19-23
22. 1 Corinthians 6:2-3
23. John 11:35
24. Mark 10:14
25. Luke 24:39
26. Revelation 22:3
27. Revelation 22:3
28. Revelation 21:4
29. Romans 6:23
30. Matthew 20:1-16
31. Ephesians 6:8
32. Mark 9:41 NIV
33. Revelation 2:23
34. Ephesians 2:10
35. 1 Corinthians 13:12
36. 1 Peter 1:12
37. Romans 8:28
38. Revelation 22:4
39. Matthew 6:25-34
40. John 14:2 NIV
41. Genesis 2:18
42. Matthew 22:30
43. Ephesians 5:32
44. John 5:23; 15:23
45. Romans 1:18–2:16
46. Revelation 21:4 ESV
47. Psalm 16:11
48. Revelation 22:3 NIV
49. Genesis 3:17-18
50. Matthew 25:23
51. Revelation 8:7-13; 15:2
52. 1 Chronicles 25:1-8;
    Psalm 150
    Mark 14:26
    Ephesians 5:19
53. Ecclesiastes 3:4
    Jeremiah 31:12-14
    Exodus 15:20-21
    2 Samuel 6:16
    Luke 15:25
54. 1 Corinthians 9:24,27
    2 Timothy 2:5
55. Luke 6:21
56. Luke 6:23
57. 2 Peter 3:13
58. John 20:19
    Luke 24:31
    Acts 1:9
59. Luke 24:41-43
60. Revelation 22:2
61. Matthew 8:11
62. Revelation 19:9
63. Revelation 21:27
64. 1 John 5:13
65. 2 Peter 3:13

PHOTOS

Presentation page — Olympic Nat'l Park, WA
Title page and cover — Lake O'Hare, Yoho Nat'l Park, Canada
Dedication page — Mt. McKinley, Denali Nat'l Park, AK
pg 4 — Napali Coast, Kauai, HI
pg 6 — Sunset at Marsh Creek Lake, PA
pg 9 — Sun sets behind Whidby Island, WA
pg 10 — Canyonlands Nat'l Park, UT
pg 13 — Clouds above Three Fingered Jack, OR
pg 15 — Clouds over Strait of Juan de Fuca from Olympic Nat'l Park, WA
pg 16 — Dusk, Columbia River, OR
pg 19 — Sunrise above clouds, Olympic Nat'l Park, WA
pg 20 — Little Redfish Lake, ID
pg 23 — Grand Teton Nat'l Park, WY
pg 24 — Mt Adams from Mt St Helens Nat'l Volcanic Monument, WA
pg 27 — Deep Lake, Wind River Wilderness, WY
pg 28 — Mt One Eye, Princess Louisa Inlet, BC, Canada
pg 30 — Austrian Alps near Brenner Pass, Austria
pg 33 — Cascade Range from Mt Hood, OR
pg 34 — The Organ, Arches Nat'l Park, UT
pg 37 — Black Butte, OR
pg 39 — Broken Top Mt and the South Sister, OR
pg 40 — Larch Valley, Banff Nat'l Park, Alberta, Canada
pg 42 — The Schreckhorn, Switzerland
pg 45 — Mt Ritter and Garnet Lake, Ansel Adams Wilderness, CA
pg 46 — Near Loch Etive, Scotland
pg 49 — Mt Rainier Nat'l Park, WA
pg 51 — Mt Hood Nat'l Forest, OR
pg 53 — Park Meadow, Three Sisters Wilderness, OR
pg 54 — Mt Hood Wilderness, OR
pg 57 — Sawtooth Lake, Sawtooth Wilderness, ID
pg 58 — Chatterbox Falls, Princess Louisa Inlet, BC, Canada
pg 61 — Toroweep Point, Grand Canyon Nat'l Park, AZ
pg 62 — Ponytail Falls, Columbia River Gorge Nat'l Scenic Area, OR
pg 64 — Yoho Nat'l Park, BC, Canada
End page — Red Rock Canyon Nat'l Conservation Area, NV

CONTACT INFORMATION:

Eternal Perspective Ministries: www.epm.org

Follow Randy Alcorn on Facebook: *www.facebook.com/randyalcorn*

Twitter: *www.twitter.com/randyalcorn*

and his blog: *www.randyalcorn.blogspot.com*